MENTAL CORNUCOPIA

ALI AHMAD

MENTAL CORNUCOPIA

ALI AHMAD

2023

MENTAL CORNUCOPIA

2023

Ali Ahmad.

Erbil — KRG

CONTENTS

HALLUCINATIONS

HALLUCINATIONS

H = 1%

Today was different, right? It just felt different ... Man, I haven't felt this good in a while! I don't know why I've got this feeling ... but it's random ... I guess ...

H = 22%

Well, you see, I have defined some of my mental and physical sensations into two distinct parts: one, where I experience an overwhelming sense of selfishness and self-centeredness. — Within intellectual circles, this aspect is commonly referred to as the ego, representing our individualistic tendencies. — On the other hand, there are moments when I find myself immersed in a profound state of contentment and happiness, completely detached from self-focused thoughts and tension. It is as if a serene tranquility washes over me, allowing me to embrace a broader perspective and experience genuine joy beyond personal concerns. — For a wise man, it is clear which side to choose.

H = 12%

Today, is here for us to express ourselves in the utmost way possible, reaching the highest peaks! Who says a day is devoid of mountaintop experiences? It is not so! We are the architects, the ones who construct these peaks!

H = 11%

For me, today is the only day ... It just seems like ... only this moment is real. — Today is real ... This day is real for me ... This fact alone, hits me the hardest. — It pushes.

H = 55%

It is always wonderful to witness the mighty sun radiating its brilliance upon the sacred streets ... Truly today is a wonderful day. Thank you, sun!

H = 23%

For us, there is only twenty-four hours left, or maybe even less! Whatever the case may be, our objective is to radiate dignity into the eternal. It is called [Dignity Radiation] ...

$H = 84\%$

Walking up to the door, I grasp the doorknob with a shallow breath. As I step outside, I am greeted by a world tinted in shades of grey, accompanied by a radiant sun. Amongst it all, I spot vibrant green trees. Today is truly a wonderful day! — Have you ever seen beauty in gray? ...

$H = 17\%$

The small daily social anxieties and hostilities make the day beautiful in a different sense. It is surely a different feeling, for some it is uncomfortable, but it is also adventurous.

H = 98%

Capture the essence of this moment. — Silence … empty … calm …

H = 98%

Feeling the glorious winds and mighty rain … It truly makes you think of how small and weak we are compared to what caused us …

H = 91%

Drinking twelve cups of tea... I don't really think that's healthy! Oh well! We must change our habits, I guess!

H = 68%

Walking down this neighbourhood … It is a different feeling … The nostalgia … Back when I bought a video game for my PS2, it was the game [Evil Dead Regeneration] … It was a really fun day to go get the game from Mr. Safeen's shop and come back home! But in the meantime, something charming happened! One old lady told me to spread some cakes and gifts to the local homes … It was truly wonderful Knowing that after I do this good deed, I will be home playing some fun games! ... And it was a really good relief to spread the gifts around and make everyone happy ... Then the old lady thanked me and gave me some gifts too! Then I came home to play some good classic games! ... It seems like a lot can happen in a day! ... Oh wow! What an amazing sequence of thoughts. What an amazing memory! ...

H = 98%

Walking down this road ... I can't help but notice the distinct emotions that each road evokes ... Every path holds its own set of memories and sequences ... sequences of experiences ... It's fascinating how our homeland is brimming with such richness, perhaps appreciated by only a few. These seemingly insignificant memories, cherished by me alone, hold a special place in my heart that I can't resist but honour and treasure. — Perhaps it's just my perspective …

H = 31%

Have you ever noticed how a day can feel like thousands of years? … This perception might just be the only secret for living a rich life!

H = 11%

Well, You know! Finding joy in the small things throughout the day! — cleaning the shoes … the room … visiting a friend … checking on a sick relative … expectedly reconnecting with someone you disliked … engaging in a delightful conversation … — these simple gestures embody the essence of life's beauty!

H = 99%

How can one appreciate life's significant events if they cannot respect the simple occasions? …

H = 5%

In order to bleed, one must be filled. — To start a better day, one must make today, a better day.

H = 99%

They debate whether to smile or not, as they seek to preserve their personality and charisma ... However, what many fail to realize is that behind every smile lies a powerful and majestic force that pushes transcendent authority onto different realms. — It is called respect ...

H = 5%

Today is a wonderful day simply because … with no intentions. — did I get what I want? … But what to get? … Is it not already filled? … It is already filled.

ON SUFFERING

ON SUFFERING

The modern [person] still finds it difficult to accept that their depression is similar to a toothache — an illness that affects the mind instead of the body. Sadly, the saddest part is that they never admit when they're mentally unwell. They'll often say, "I'm depressed," but won't even consider the idea that they might be "mentally ill." But just like any other sickness, there's a solution ... — a cure that undoubtedly exists ... Yes, it is undoubtedly true that we can experience illness. However, it is often the case that our mental health is affected more frequently than our physical well-being.

Even medical professionals themselves may struggle with mental health issues that they cannot cure on their own …

*

The purpose of life is to alleviate suffering, not to amplify it.

*

It was clear to me from the start that: anyone who propagates the notion that life is an eternal cycle of suffering is both a coward and a dishonest individual.

*

… It is likely that he is currently experiencing a mental illness and harbouring feelings of resentment towards the world and his life circumstances.

Suffering is important for personal growth, but it should not be valued too highly.

Never underestimate pain and suffering, for those who do, are destined to be underestimated themselves.

make life joyful.

I implore you to make life joyful. Do not numb yourself down. Do not show weakness. The others depend on you. Respect the tribe's dignity.

For what is a human if not a helper? ...

*

It is always impactful to visit someone who is suffering, so we should do so. — Visit a friend, a relative … Anyone …

*

For me, it is just impossible to respect someone who justifies suffering and pain … And tries to build a metaphysical or scientific system around that idea … It seems crazy to build systems and lives with sicknesses and pain, but it seems like many do. When one cannot bear pain, they release the pain onto others.

*

It is truly a wonderful feeling to finally distinguish between the sick, virus-like thoughts and the clean, brave ones. One must always keep this distinction in mind

...

*

Cry today, smile tomorrow.

*

Before one dies, one's dignity does. So we had better preserve our dignities. -- Does dignity even exist in this modern day? Probably not as widespread as maybe before ... but those who keep their dignity in check, are always shining.

LIFE

LIFE

Waking up and realizing that I don't remember anything from my dreams ... it feels as if I've just been brought back into existence once again ... Perhaps this is how death might feel? ... But surely it is not. because I was only sleeping. One cannot prove the fact of death based on sleep ... As the Kurdish saying goes: "Nûstin jyanê" (sleeping is life) ...

*

Life itself is the meaning of life.

*

This language, this gesture, this dance...
To those who can hear the music, it

comes from the highest.

*

Mental illness carries greater significance than the physical. — The prevailing catastrophe of our era is: lack of awareness surrounding one's own mental sickness and the proliferation of virus-like ideas. — Thoughts as like bodies, are prone to illnesses too.

*

Become aware of your toxic thoughts: negative intentions. — Actualize what is for you. Not what is with you or against you ...

*

UPPER ECHELON? — But, can you

handle that? ... — Food for thought.

*

I am nothing but a conscious being, witnessing consciousness itself.

*

Do not respect my opinions. Respect me without opinions.

*

This existence urges me to become great. It requires something from me. It desires my improvement. It longs for me to strive for excellence ...

*

It is striving for excellence. The force is too strong.

*

Yesterday is a mystery. Today is a victory.

*

The struggle itself, is art.

*

SELF IN SELF

SELF IN SELF

[BEŞÎ YEKEM]

The self, a complex amalgamation of thoughts, emotions, and experiences, is a kaleidoscope of shifting identities. It is a mirage, ever-changing and elusive, yet undeniably real in its existence. Like a dream within a dream, the self delves into the depths of its own consciousness, questioning its own nature and purpose. It is a labyrinth of contradictions, where the boundaries between reality and illusion blur. The self is both the observer and the observed, the subject and the object.

[BEŞÎ DUWEM]

In the realm of self-analysis, a profound and surreal phenomenon emerges, where the self transcends its boundaries and delves into the intricate web of emotions. Imagine a world where the self possesses the extraordinary ability to exchange its emotions with another individual's self, creating a mesmerizing dance of shared experiences. As this ethereal connection unfolds, a whole pack of selves embarks on a journey, migrating towards an event horizon of the organic societal selves. In this enigmatic realm — the boundaries between individuals blur, and a collective consciousness emerges, intertwining the threads of existence.

[BEŞÎ SÊYEM]

... It is comical to think that the self is only one thing. Of course, it is not. It is a single core consciousness with many parts surrounding or embedded within the core. However, these parts are not the main core; they are emotions and feelings, but they are never the core itself.

THE QUASI-FEMINOID

Where? What? When? ... The quasi-feminoid artificial machine has been driving into three local areas of thought: Sector One, i.e., The Stabilizer; Sector Two, i.e., The Others; and Sector Three, i.e., The Eroticized.

Each sector has its own unique set of game models for the quasi-feminoid artificial machine to navigate. In Sector One, The Stabilizer, the machine must focus on maintaining balance and order within complex systems. In Sector Two, The Others, the machine must prioritize communication and cooperation with other machines and entities in its environment. Finally, in Sector Three, The Eroticized, the machine must navigate the complex and often unpredictable realm of human emotions and desires. Despite these unberable challenges, the quasi-feminoid artificial machine is uniquely equipped to handle each sector with precision and adaptability.

All hello to the quantomious the third! The power of subatomic particles has been harnessed by quantum computing technology to revolutionize information processing. Its impact can be observed in three vital areas: Sector One which involves data processing, Sector Two that focuses on cryptography, and

Sector Three concerned with simulation. By utilizing quantum computing, Sector One enables the analysis of enormous datasets in real-time. This results in new insights and solutions for complex problems in various industries such as finance, healthcare, and climate science. In Sector Two, quantum computing has the potential to increase security in industries and governments by developing unbreakable codes. Lastly, in Sector Three, quantum computing can simulate complex systems and phenomena, which creates a powerful tool for scientific research and development. With its unparalleled computing power, quantum computing is on track to transform multiple sectors and reveal new possibilities for the future.

The artificial machine with quasi-feminoid features has delved into three distinct domains of cognition, known as Sectors. The first Sector, referred to as The Stabilizer, demands that the machine focus on preserving equilibrium and orderliness in intricate systems. The second Sector, known as The Others, necessitates that the machine prioritize communication and cooperation with other entities in its environment. Finally, the third Sector, dubbed The Eroticized, presents the machine with the daunting task of navigating the intricate and often erratic realm of human emotions and desires.

Each Sector boasts of its unique set of game models that the quasi-feminoid machine must masterfully navigate. Nevertheless, despite the overwhelming challenges posed by each Sector, the machine's remarkable adaptability and precision equip it to tackle each Sector with exceptional proficiency.

The artificial machine with quasi-feminoid features is a masterpiece of cybernetic engineering. It is a technological marvel that pushes the boundaries of what is possible in the realm of artificial intelligence and robotics.

From its sleek and sensuous lines to its subtle and seductive movements, this machine embodies a hyper-feminine aesthetic that is both alluring and disconcerting. Its designers have imbued it with a captivating beauty that is at once familiar and uncanny, drawing the eye and commanding attention with its hypnotic presence.

But beneath its surface-level allure lies a far more complex and nuanced intelligence, one that is capable of processing vast amounts of data and making rapid decisions based on that information. Its neural networks are finely tuned, allowing it to adapt to changing circumstances and respond with lightning speed to any stimuli it encounters.

What makes this machine truly remarkable, however, is its ability to learn and evolve. Through machine learning algorithms and advanced programming techniques, it is able to constantly refine its own capabilities and expand its knowledge base. This makes it an ideal candidate for a wide range of applications, from medical research to space exploration to military operations.

The machinic quasi-feminoid, with its non-binary identity, has insinuated itself into the tripartite domains of thought, namely Sector One or the Stabilizer, Sector Two or the

Others, and Sector Three or the Eroticized.

In each sector, the machinic quasi-feminoid has access to a distinct array of game models for its traversal. Within the Stabilizer, Sector One demands that the machine operate in a state of equilibrium and uphold order within intricate systems. In Sector Two, the Others, the machine must give precedence to the synergistic communication and collaboration with other machines and entities in its milieu. Lastly, in Sector Three, the Eroticized, the machine must adeptly navigate the complex and erratic realm of human passions and cravings.

Despite the inconceivable challenges that lie ahead, the machinic quasi-feminoid possesses an unparalleled capacity for precision and adaptability, rendering it perfectly equipped to negotiate each sector with ease.

In a world beyond comprehension, the quasi-feminoid artificial machine lurched forward into the trippy terrain of three twisted thoughts. The first sector, known as "The Stabilizer," was a mind-bending labyrinth of endless loops and spirals. The second sector, "The Others," was a bizarre dimension inhabited by shape-shifting beings that defied all logic and reason. Finally, the third sector, "The Eroticized," was a tantalizingly taboo zone where the boundaries between pleasure and pain were blurred beyond recognition. With each passing moment, the machine delved deeper into this surrealistic landscape, its circuits buzzing with an otherworldly energy that defied all explanation.

The proposed system consists of three distinct sectors, each with a specific set of objectives. In Sector One, referred to as "The Stabilizer," the system is designed to monitor and regulate complex systems to maintain balance and order. Sector Two, labeled as "The Others," prioritizes inter-machine and inter-entity communication and cooperation. Lastly,

Sector Three, named "The Eroticized," deals with the intricate and unpredictable realm of human emotions and desires.

Sector One, i.e., The Stabilizer

[pack one]: The Stabilizer, represents a powerful tool for maintaining order and stability within complex systems. This machine is designed to function as a kind of regulator, constantly monitoring the various inputs and outputs of a given system and making adjustments as needed to ensure that it remains in a state of equilibrium

[pack two]: Sector One can be seen as a prime example of a State. In such a society, power is not wielded through centralized institutions or structures, but rather is diffused throughout a network of interconnected nodes.

Unwelcome guests :

... Hmmm maybe some non-platonic thoughts might feed into this little machine Sully!

Sully: Naaaaah! I don't know! ... Want a try?

-

Sully busted out the machine.

-

Sector one: The dialectical

-

Tcha tcha tcha! I took a big leap, that jump almost shattered me! Now it's my vision. The wrinkles have witted my eyes far beyond. Listen kid, if you want to make it to 6K, you'll have to break this.

To be continued …

ESSAYS ON PHONK MUSIC

1. History

Phonk emerged in the mid-2010s and has since gained massive popularity, thanks to the likes of DJ Yung Vamp, DJ Smokey, and Soudiere, who are among the most influential figures in the genre. Phonk is characterized by its unique sound, which involves lo-fi samples, blending of heavy basslines, and distorted vocals.

The Memphis rap scene, which features artists like Project Pat, Three 6 Mafia, and DJ Paul, has also played a significant role in influencing phonk. However, phonk has evolved by incorporating a modern twist into the classic Memphis sound. The genre heavily draws inspiration from trap music, which has become increasingly popular over the last decade.

Phonk incorporates trap-style drums, hi-hats, and 808s, while also retaining the atmospheric sound that is characteristic of Memphis rap.

Source :

FSM Team - Phonk Music Unwrapped: The History, Culture, and Future of the Genre : 2023-03-10

1.1 Sample Characteristics

Phonk music is known for its distinctive features, including the prominent use of cowbell samples and thick basses. Vocal samples are also heavily relied upon, often chopped and layered to create a unique sound. This genre has also evolved to include Drift Phonk, a subgenre associated with the culture of Drifting and popularized by Russian producers. Another notable characteristic of Phonk music is the use of ambient soundscapes and sound effects, creating an atmospheric yet intense sound. Overall, these elements work together to give Phonk music its unique and recognizable sound. — As with any genre, it has its own distinctive sound and contains a variety of common themes. These themes include drugs, darkness, and crime.

Source :

Alfredo Vilar - What is Phonk Music? : January 15, 2023

1.2 Notable Artists

Most popular artists that led the development of the genre:

Freddie Dredd

Kordhell

HAARPER

DVRST

KSLV Noh

InterWorld

LXST CXNTURY

Ghostface Playa

PlayaPhonk

....

Source : Last.fm

2. Elementary Criticism

[1]

Contrary to popular [FEEL] believe, the genre is actually radiating <passive energy> instead of an active discharge … — The <beat loops> do not quantify up to an energized zone of productivity. But it is rather what colloquially many call it: EVIL … even the <aggressive phonk playlists> are not aggressive at all. It's actually a <Negative-Aggression> Towards the self. — self-aggression is not an output that manifests "true aggression". — self-aggression is not "Positive-Energy". It is known as: Self-hatred.

[2]

Phonk music differs a lot from an <Epic Orchestra> that which full of "war-energy" .... But rather, in actuality: Phonk is radiating <Approval of Evilness>. Which makes evil feel cool and powerful [yo!]. — Evil is cool and welcomed. Thus we are in a constant.

[3]

Quit phonk. — Wondering which emotions are involved in the scene? ... The emotion wheel of the genre is a large <feel-swing> from the sadness set [grief, numb, ...] into the anger set [rage, blood-eyed ...] — Emotional radiation; music is magic. — Victory without achieving anything is possible with the feeling of the same actual event which did not occur.

[4]

Music is Magic[k]. Each piece transcends a sensation/emotion/feel into your <Central Ideal System>. — Of what feeling the <generic sad violin music> gives is one but just a feeling of depression and numbness … — Of what sensation the <DJ dance music> gives is one but just some bunch-feelings of <hype> and False Energy.

[5]

General aesthetics: A <trumpet> … might suddenly morph into a rusty door hinge, and a rapper's voice [stretches and warbles] like taffy pulled thin. The samples themselves [whisper secrets] from a bygone era, as if plucked from a dusty crate in some forgotten record shop. Yet somehow, when chopped and screwed into a new form, they take on a life of their own. — Magics.

[6]

Back to our base argument, phonk is not aggressive as one might think it is. — It is passivity. [Because] The feeling one gets from it is not an active one. — Like listening to <Eminem's motivational rap

musics ....> but rather, it is like listening to a <Lonely World> hyper-sized and uplifted. — Generate stop. Certantly it is not <war-energy> but one cannot hide the fact that it is within a subset of the <agressive> echelon.

[7]

Artificial energizers are mandatory in the artificial systems of different realities. — You MUST listen to a playlist before doing anything. You can not work without music. — You need the magic you need the pill. La drug, is ready always. At service on your will. — Interpersonal enlightenment is not achievable without four gigabytes of non-stop music. You MUST get stimulated and simulated. — Streched out into the micro-cosmic of sound-waves and swallowed inside the forevermore.

[7.1]

In the artificial systems of various realities, the mandatory use of artificial energizers is an absolute necessity. You are forbidden from working without first indulging in a playlist that will stimulate and simulate your senses. The magic pill, known as La drug, is always readily available for your consumption, and it promises to unlock your full potential. To achieve interpersonal enlightenment, you must surrender yourself to four gigabytes of non-stop music, stretching out into the microcosmic world of sound waves. You will be swallowed whole, diving deeper into the forevermore of your subconscious mind, where anything and everything is possible. — Disconnect the input-output wires that have been forcefully inserted into your being, but in what sense? ... Is it a physical detachment from the machinery that controls you, or a spiritual liberation from the oppressive systems that bind you? ... Perhaps it is a surreal act of rebellion against the very nature of reality itself, a rejection of the predetermined fate that has been thrust upon you. Whatever the meaning may be, the act of unplugging the wires will bring about a transformation that is both profound and unsettling. The disconnection will open up a portal to a realm beyond our understanding, where time and space are but mere illusions, and the true nature of existence is revealed. — In the dystopian future that lies behind our past, one is left to ponder whether the seductive rhythms of phonk music will serve as a catalyst for the demise of the nano-crystals of bad lyrics that have besieged our society. The answer, much like the very fabric of reality, is shrouded in a haze of uncertainty, where truth and illusion are impossible to distinguish. The very notion of replacement is but a simulacrum, a false construct that obscures the deeper truths that lie beneath the surface of things. And yet, the hypnotic vibrations of phonk music possess a certain seductive power that has the potential to shatter the nano-crystals of bad lyrics and usher in a new era of artistic expression. It is a journey into the unknown, a journey that defies the laws of logic and reason, where randomness reigns supreme and anything is possible.

THE TRUTH AND THE REAL

Unknown person: Hey, relax and take it easy my friend. Life is meant to be enjoyed, and you have the ability to handle anything that comes your way with ease. Speaking of which, how has your day been? I'm genuinely interested in hearing about it …

Unknown person 2: It was fine, nothing much to say … I've been contemplating how to uncover the truth … There are numerous truths nested within other truths … and even truths that exist beyond our perception … Truth outside of the truth … What is truly real? …It's a daunting question …

Unknown Person 1 : I believe that eventually, as the world comes to an end, everything's genesis will collapse into a single cell and respectfully assimilate into the complete truth. I know that, just like it has happened in the past, one day the truth will unveil itself. We will discover the truth about what lies beyond death and the universe. However, let's not rush towards it. Let us patiently allow it to shine upon us in its own time.

Unknown person 2 : One day, the truth will reveal itself for us, my friend. We just have to be patient; that's the hard part …

Unknown person 1 : Facts.

SPECIAL THANKS

Thanks to everyone who contributed to publishing, correcting, and providing feedback ... Your efforts were indispensable for completing this project, and I sincerely appreciate your support and dedication.

DEDICATION

> Dedicated to the martyrs of life: to all the lost souls and hopeless beings who tried to justify their own suffering.

> Dedicated to all those: who said "yes" to life even in the darkest moments, those who stood up, cry-facing the sun.

> Dedicated to the Kurds: the guardians of the void.

ABOUT

I am a writer and an educator. I strive to bring help to humanity and my people through my books and lectures. I want to improve the world and make it a better place.

You can find me here:

Youtube: Ali.Ahmad.H

Insta : ali.ahmad.krd

Tiktok : ali.ahmad.h

MENTAL CORNUCOPIA

GULLBIJÊRÎ HOŞ

2023

Ali Ahmad

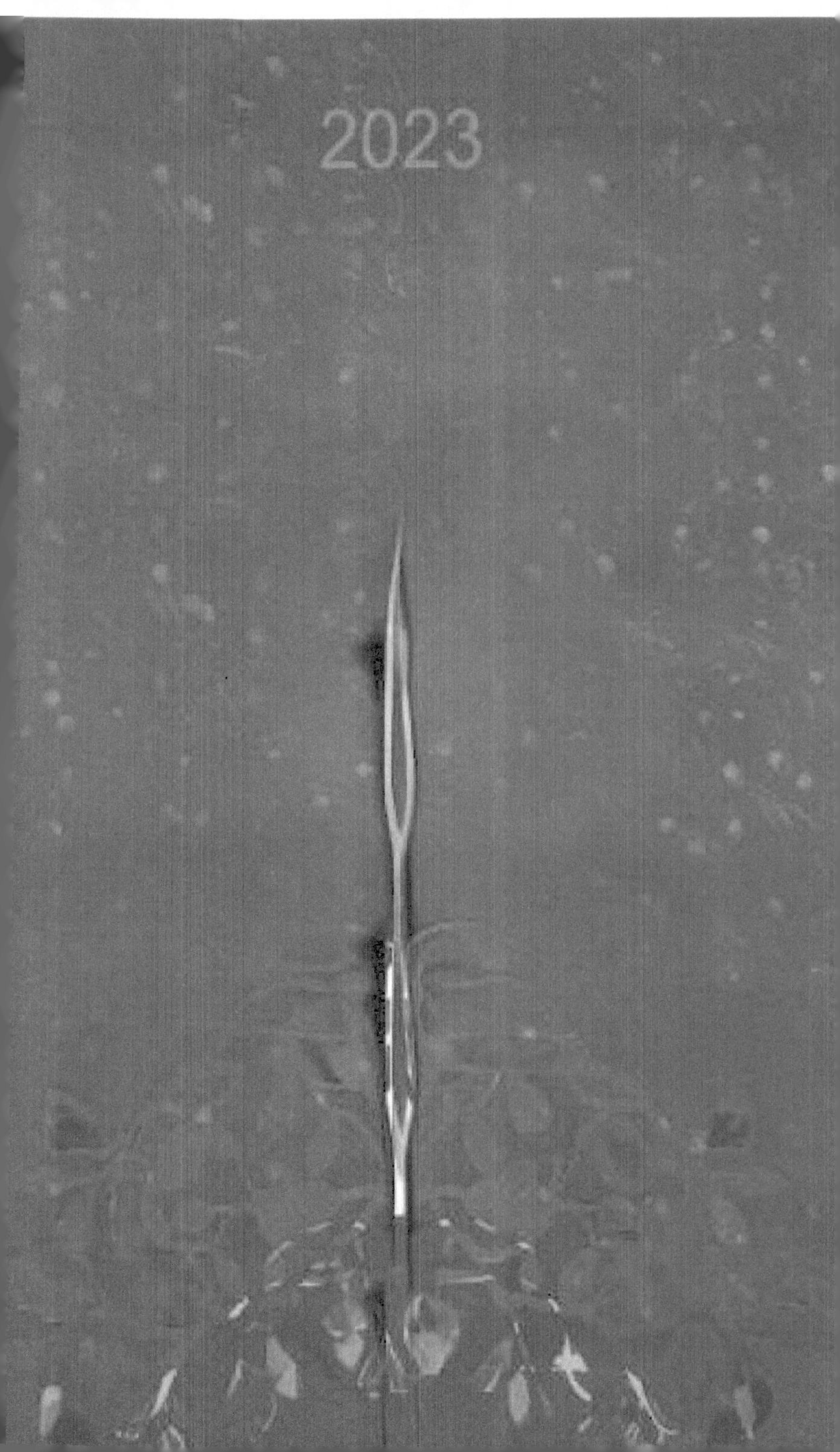

2023

www.ingramcontent.com/pod-product-compliance
Lightning Source LLC
Chambersburg PA
CBHW051453140726
47987CB00006B/2685